my Book 3

Authors and Advisors

Alma Flor Ada • Kylene Beers • F. Isabel Campoy
Joyce Armstrong Carroll • Nathan Clemens
Anne Cunningham • Martha C. Hougen
Elena Izquierdo • Carol Jago • Erik Palmer
Robert E. Probst • Shane Templeton • Julie Washington

Contributing Consultants

David Dockterman • Mindset Works®
Jill Eggleton

Printed in the U.S.A.

ISBN   978-1-328-51694-7

6 7 8 9 10   0868   27 26 25 24 23 22 21

4500817730   C D E F G

into Reading™

myBook 3

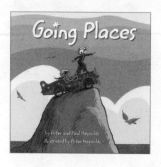
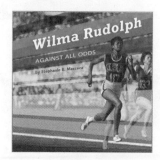

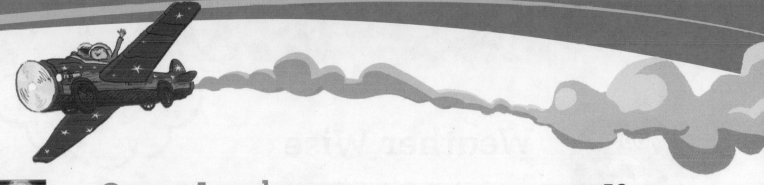

Lead the Way

"Great leaders have to think
outside the box sometimes."

—Rick Riordan

What are the qualities of a good leader?

Get Curious Video

Words About Leadership

Complete the Vocabulary Network to show what you know
about the words.

admire

Meaning: When you **admire** someone, you like and respect that person.

Synonyms and Antonyms	Drawing

inspire

Meaning: When people **inspire** you, they give you new ideas.

Synonyms and Antonyms	Drawing

pioneer

Meaning: When you **pioneer** something, you are the first person to do it.

Synonyms and Antonyms	Drawing

What's Good to Read?
Book Reviews for Kids by Kids!

BOOK: *Emmanuel Ofosu Yeboah:*
What Makes a Great Leader?
by Malikah Hansen

GENRE: Biography

REVIEWER: Ruthie Miller

AGE: 8

I think this biography is terrific! It is about a man from Ghana whose leg didn't form properly before he was born. Many people thought he would have a hard life because of his leg. He proved them wrong and became a leader!

I like this book because it shows what happens when people believe in themselves. For example, some people said Emmanuel wouldn't be able to do things like go to school or play sports. Emmanuel had other ideas. He hopped to and from school each day. He learned to play soccer and how to ride a bike.

Another thing I like about the book is that it is about a special kind of leader. Emmanuel set an example for others. He changed how they think. In 2001, Emmanuel rode his bike across Ghana. He showed that people with disabilities can do amazing things.

This book reminds you that everyone is special and can become a leader just like Emmanuel did. Everyone should read it!

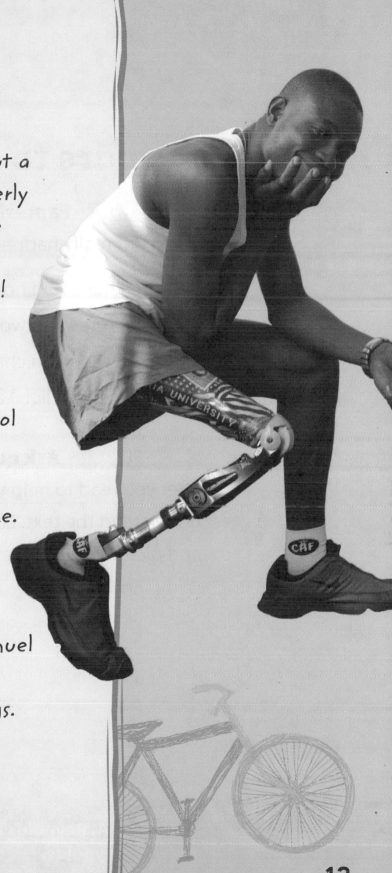

Prepare to Read

GENRE STUDY **Fantasies** are stories with made-up events that could not really happen. As you read *Going Places*, look for:

- events that could not happen in real life
- how pictures and words help you understand what happens
- a lesson the main character learns
- problems (conflicts) and solutions (resolutions)

SET A PURPOSE **Ask questions** before, during, and after you read to help you get information or understand the text. Look for evidence in the text and pictures to **answer** your questions.

POWER WORDS

assured

exactly

precise

peered

respond

intent

contraption

replica

Meet Paul A. Reynolds and Peter H. Reynolds.

Going Places

by Peter and Paul Reynolds

illustrated by Peter Reynolds

Rafael had been waiting all year
long for the **Going Places** contest, a
chance to build a go-cart, race it . . .
and win.

When their teacher announced,
"Who would like the first kit?"
Rafael's hand shot up.

The rest of the class watched enviously as Rafael walked back to his seat with a kit.

Mrs. Chanda assured them, "Don't worry—you'll all be getting one . . .

...and they're all EXACTLY alike."

The kit came with a set of precise instructions.
That made Rafael happy. He was very good at
following directions.

Rafael hammered, glued, nailed, and assembled his kit.

His go-cart looked just like the one in the directions. He was feeling quite proud.

Rafael wondered how his classmate Maya was doing. She lived right next door.

He peered over the fence. "Hey, Maya, you haven't even started?!"

Maya didn't respond. She was so intent on watching the bird in front of her, and quickly sketching it, that she didn't even notice Rafael.

Then she just put down her pencil
and stared at the bird dreamily.

Rafael shrugged—and let her be.

The next morning Rafael checked back in to see how Maya was doing.

"Wow, what is that?" he asked.

Maya grinned. "You like it?"

Rafael responded slowly, "Yeeeaah—extremely cool. But, uh, Maya, there's just one little problem. That's not a go-cart."

Maya smiled. "Who said it HAD to be a go-cart?"

Rafael was confused. The set of instructions inside the box were for a GO-CART. But then again, they didn't say it HAD to be a go-cart. He looked again at Maya's contraption. After a moment, he grinned.

"I get it. Hey, Maya, I really want to win this race. The instructions never said we couldn't team up either!"

And so they did, working late into the evening.

The next day everyone gathered for the big race.
Each go-cart was a perfect replica of the other.

25

Except one.

One of the kids laughed. "Looks like you had trouble with the **Going Places** instructions. You're going places all right—you're GOING to lose!"

Maya and Rafael didn't even have time to respond because the announcer's big, boomy voice called out,

ATTENTION RACERS!
START YOUR ENGINES!
4...3...2...1...

A buzzer sounded.

"And they're off!"

While all the other go-carts disappeared in a cloud of dust, Maya just sat there in their motionless vehicle. Rafael shouted over the roar of engines and cheering crowds. "Maya! What are we waiting for?"

"No worries, Rafael!" Maya answered. "Flaps down, throttle up!"

And now THEY took off—off into the air!

The other contestants looked up in amazement.

Maya and Rafael hovered and then sped past them all.

Before long, Maya and Rafael
coasted across the finish line to the
cheers of the waiting crowd.

They kept rolling clear across the race grounds.
Maya slammed the brakes, stopping just short
of the lake at the edge of the school field.

Rafael noticed a startled frog leap from a lily
pad and dive into the water. He raised his eyebrow
and looked at Maya. She smiled.

"Rafael, are you thinking
what I'm thinking . . . ?"

Rafael just nodded.

 Turn and Talk

Use details from *Going Places* to answer these questions with a partner.

1. **Ask and Answer Questions** What questions did you ask yourself about the story before, during, and after reading? How did your questions help you understand the story?

2. Why do the kids laugh when they first see Rafael and Maya's vehicle? How do their feelings change after the race begins?

3. What do you think Rafael learns from this experience?

Talking Tip

Ask a question if you are not sure about your partner's ideas.

Why did you say _____?

Write a Victory Speech

PROMPT What would Maya and Rafael say in a victory speech after the race? Look for details in the words and pictures about how they won and how it makes them feel.

PLAN First, write three details that explain why Maya and Rafael won the race.

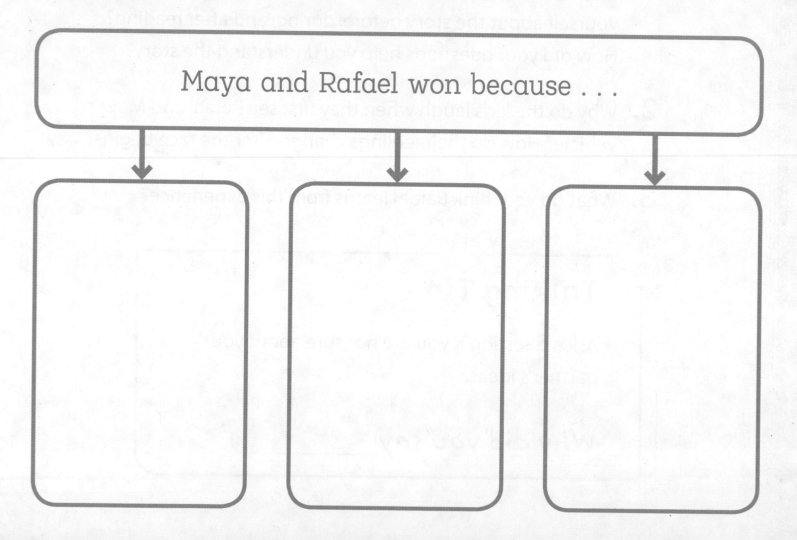

Maya and Rafael won because . . .

Going Places
by Peter and Paul Reynolds
illustrated by Peter Reynolds

WRITE Now use what you know about Maya and Rafael to write their victory speech. Remember to:

- Include exciting details from the race.

- At the end, thank the audience for listening.

_____

_____

_____

_____

_____

_____

_____

_____

_____

_____

_____

Prepare to Read

GENRE STUDY **Fantasies** are stories with made-up events that could not really happen.

MAKE A PREDICTION Preview "Captain Cat Keeps Her Cool." This cat has a team to lead. You know that most stories include a problem. What problem do you think the team will have?

_____

_____

_____

_____

_____

_____

SET A PURPOSE Read to find out how Captain Cat leads her team and to see if your prediction is right. If not, think about what you know about story structure and make a new prediction.

Captain Cat Keeps Her Cool

READ What questions can you ask yourself about Captain Cat?

At last the rain stopped. The animals had been cooped up all day. Now they could finally go outside and play!

"To the playing field!" Rooster and Horse yelled.

"Wait," Mouse squcakcd. "What if the field is flooded?"

"Don't be silly," Cow answered. "Moooooove!"

Mouse didn't move, though. Rooster, Horse, and Cow stopped, too. Then they all looked at Captain Cat. Captain Cat was not big and strong, but she was fair and good at solving problems. She would know just what to do.

> **Close Reading Tip**
>
> Is your prediction right so far? If not, make a new prediction.

READ What do you learn about Captain Cat?

"Team, let's get organized," Captain Cat began. "Cow and Mouse, you are in charge of warm-up exercises. Horse and Rooster, you lead the team song. I'll go check out the field."

The animals got busy right away. When Captain Cat returned, they were exercising and singing happily. Captain Cat announced that the field was not flooded at all. All the animals cheered and ran to the field together.

"Are you ready to play?" yelled Captain Cat with a grin.

"Let's play ball!" the animals exclaimed with glee.

Close Reading Tip

Circle words you don't know. Then figure them out. If you need to, look them up in a dictionary.

CHECK MY UNDERSTANDING

How is the problem in the story solved? How does the story end?

_____

_____

_____

_____

_____

WRITE ABOUT IT Is Captain Cat a good leader? Why or why not? Use details from the story in your answer.

_____

_____

_____

_____

_____

_____

_____

_____

_____

_____

Prepare to Read

GENRE STUDY **Biographies** tell about real people's lives. As you read *Wilma Rudolph: Against All Odds*, notice:

- what the person did
- photos of the person
- a timeline that shows order of events

SET A PURPOSE Read to find out the most important ideas in each part. Then **synthesize,** or put together these ideas in your mind, to find out what the text really means to you.

POWER WORDS

rare

relay

honored

success

Build Background: The Olympics: Track and Field Events

Wilma Rudolph

AGAINST ALL ODDS

by Stephanie E. Macceca

Little Wilma

Wilma Rudolph was born on June 23, 1940, in Tennessee (ten-uh-SEE). She was born early. She only weighed 4.5 pounds. She was often sick because she was so small.

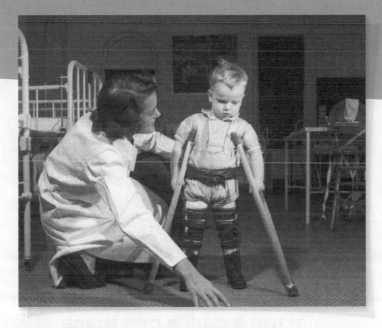

Some children with polio learn to walk with braces and crutches.

President Franklin D. Roosevelt had polio. He could not walk. Today polio is very rare. People can get shots so they do not get polio.

Polio

At age four, Wilma was very sick. She got better. But, her mother was still worried. Something was wrong with her left leg and foot. The doctor said Wilma had polio (POH-lee-oh).

The doctor said Wilma would never walk. Wilma could not walk for two years. Her brothers and sisters helped her by exercising her left foot and leg.

Wilma wore a brace on her leg. She could not play games and sports at school. She watched the other kids play. She wanted to be like them.

Wilma's high school picture

Sports

Wilma worked hard to get stronger. By age 12, she did not use a crutch or a brace. Wilma was happy to play sports. Her brothers built a basketball hoop in their backyard. They taught Wilma how to play.

Wilma wanted to play basketball in high school. The coach wanted her sister on the team. Wilma's dad said both girls had to play. The coach agreed. Wilma became a star player!

Coach Ed Temple

Ed Temple was a college track coach. He saw Wilma play basketball. He thought Wilma could be a track star. He let Wilma practice with his college track team. Wilma practiced hard. She wanted to get better.

At first, Wilma was not a fast runner. Coach Temple showed her some special tricks to run faster.

FUN FACT

Wilma scored the most points in a state basketball championship.

Wilma and teammates train for the 1960 Olympics.

The Olympics

Wilma's hard work paid off. At age 16, she made it to the Olympics (uh-LIM-piks) for track and field. She won the bronze medal for the 100-meter relay race.

Wilma training for a race

Wilma and President John F. Kennedy   **Wilma in a parade**

No one thought Wilma's team would win a medal in the 1956 Olympics.

Wilma was proud of her bronze medal. But she wanted to win a gold medal. Wilma set goals. She worked hard for four years.

In 1960, Wilma went to the Olympics again. She ran in three races. She won every one. She was the first American woman to win three gold medals at one Olympics!

FUN FACT

Wilma was called "The Tennessee Tornado" and "The Black Pearl."

Wilma holding her college diploma

Wilma received an award with her hero, Jesse Owens, on the right.

A True Hero

After the 1960 Olympics, Wilma went to college. She became a teacher and a coach. Wilma won many awards, too. She was one of the first African American women to be honored for being a good athlete.

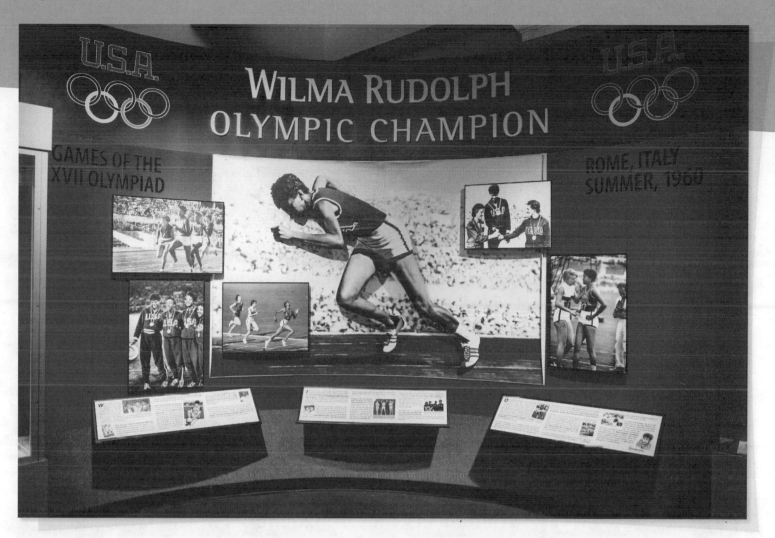

A display to honor Wilma is in a museum in Tennessee.

Wilma's success gave many women a chance to try new things. Sadly, Wilma died young on November 12, 1994. But her amazing work will never be forgotten.

FUN FACT

In 2004, the United States Postal Service created a stamp to honor Wilma.

Timeline

1940 — Wilma Rudolph is born in Tennessee.

1944 — Wilma is diagnosed with polio.

1952 — Wilma learns to play basketball and walk without help from a crutch or a brace.

1956 — Wilma wins the bronze medal at the Olympics.

1960 — Wilma becomes the first American woman to win three gold medals at the Olympics.

1994 — Wilma dies at the age of 54.

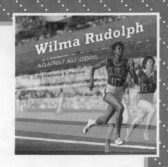

Use details from *Wilma Rudolph: Against All Odds* to answer these questions with a partner.

1. **Synthesize** The events in Wilma's life took place long ago. Why is her story still important to people today?

2. What problems did Wilma face as a child?

3. Why do you think the author included a timeline on the last page? How can you use the timeline to find and understand information about Wilma Rudolph?

Listening Tip

Wait until your partner has finished speaking before asking a question or adding new information.

Write Advice

PROMPT What advice do you think Wilma Rudolph would give about believing in yourself? Use details from the text and photographs to explain your ideas.

PLAN First, make notes about the challenges Wilma Rudolph faced. Then make notes about her accomplishments.

Challenges	Accomplishments

WRITE Now write the advice you think Wilma Rudolph would give about believing in yourself. Remember to:

- Include details from her life that support your ideas.

- Use words like *I believe* or *I feel*.

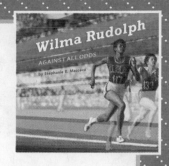

_____

_____

_____

_____

_____

_____

_____

_____

_____

_____

_____

Prepare to Read

GENRE STUDY **Biographies** tell about real people's lives.

MAKE A PREDICTION Preview "Standing Up for Migrant Workers."
Cesar Chavez worked hard to help others. Read the title and the
headings. What do you think he did?

_____

_____

_____

_____

_____

_____

SET A PURPOSE Read to find out why Cesar Chavez was admired
by migrant workers.

Standing Up for Migrant Workers

READ What was Cesar Chavez's childhood like?

Childhood Years

Cesar Chavez was born in 1927 in Arizona. In 1939, his family moved to California. They became migrant farm workers. That means they moved from farm to farm to pick fruits and vegetables. It was a difficult way of life. They worked long hours for low pay. To help his family, Chavez quit school after the eighth grade to work on farms full-time. ▶

Close Reading Tip

Number the main events in order.

CHECK MY UNDERSTANDING

Why do you think the author includes the heading "Childhood Years"?

_____

_____

55

READ How did Cesar Chavez help others?

Close Reading Tip

Underline the heading. Was your prediction about Cesar Chavez correct? What was different?

Helping Farm Workers

Cesar Chavez wanted people to know about the farm workers' long hours and low pay. He also wanted laws to help them. In the 1960s, he led many peaceful marches. The marches brought attention to his cause.

Chavez continued to fight. After many years, his hard work made a difference. Migrant workers were given better pay and hours. Chavez died in 1993. He is admired by people everywhere because he fought for human rights.

CHECK MY UNDERSTANDING

Why are the events in Cesar's life still important today?

_____

_____

_____

_____

WRITE ABOUT IT Why do you think Cesar Chavez is an important leader to know about? Use details from the text to explain your answer.

_____

_____

_____

_____

_____

_____

_____

_____

_____

_____

_____

Prepare to Read

GENRE STUDY **Opinion writing** shows an author's thoughts, beliefs, or ideas. When you read *Great Leaders*, look for:

- what the author's opinion is
- reasons that support an opinion
- ways the author tries to make the reader agree with him or her

SET A PURPOSE As you read, think about the author's words. Then **evaluate,** or decide, which details are most important to help you understand the text.

POWER WORDS

politics

advice

earned

equal

Build Background: Having Opinions

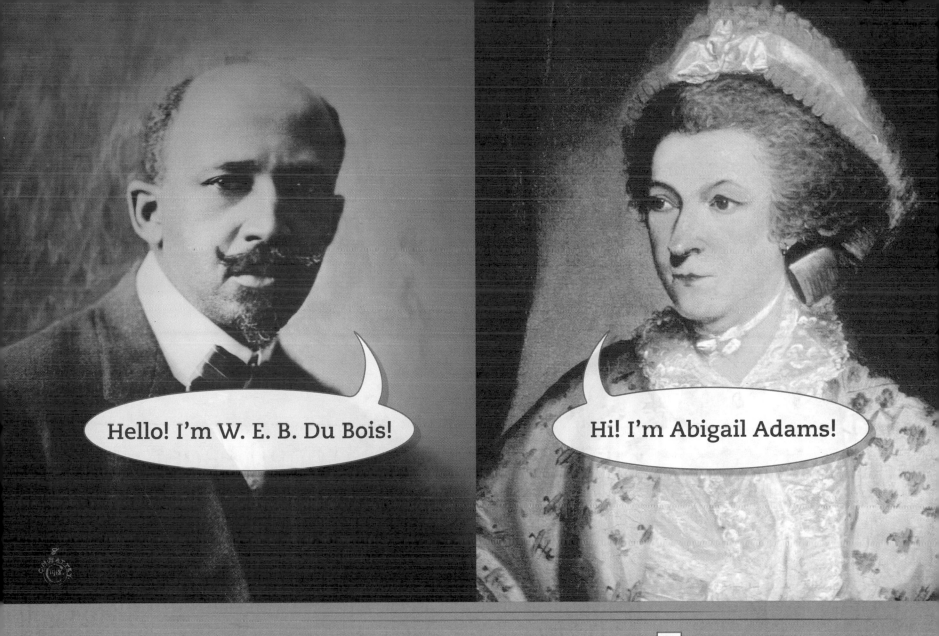

Great Leaders

The school newspaper asked two students to write their opinions about a great leader in history. Olivia chose Abigail Adams. Anthony chose W. E. B. Du Bois. Read both essays. What makes each person a great leader?

Hi! I'm Olivia!

Abigail and John Adams

ABIGAIL ADAMS:
Strong Woman, Strong Leader
by Olivia

Abigail Adams was a strong leader. She was focused on getting things done. I hope you will agree with me!

Abigail was the wife of our second president, John Adams. Many women didn't have a good education then. Abigail couldn't go to school when she was little because of illness. She was very smart, though. She learned things on her own. She studied history and politics.

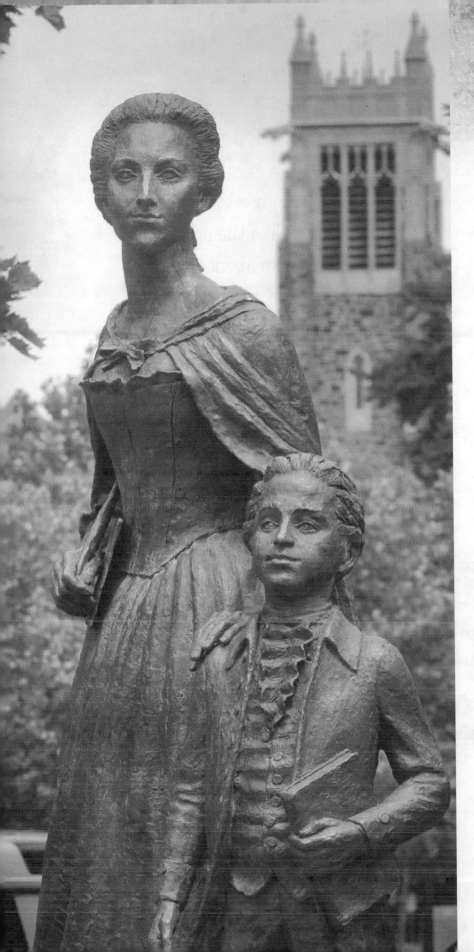

When John was away, Abigail took care of her normal chores. She did John's chores, too! She even bought and sold land. Back then, only men did those types of jobs.

Abigail felt strongly about women's rights. As the United States was forming, she wrote a letter to John. She wanted him to tell the men to "remember the ladies." She felt women should help make the laws if they had to follow them.

Statue of Abigail Adams and her son

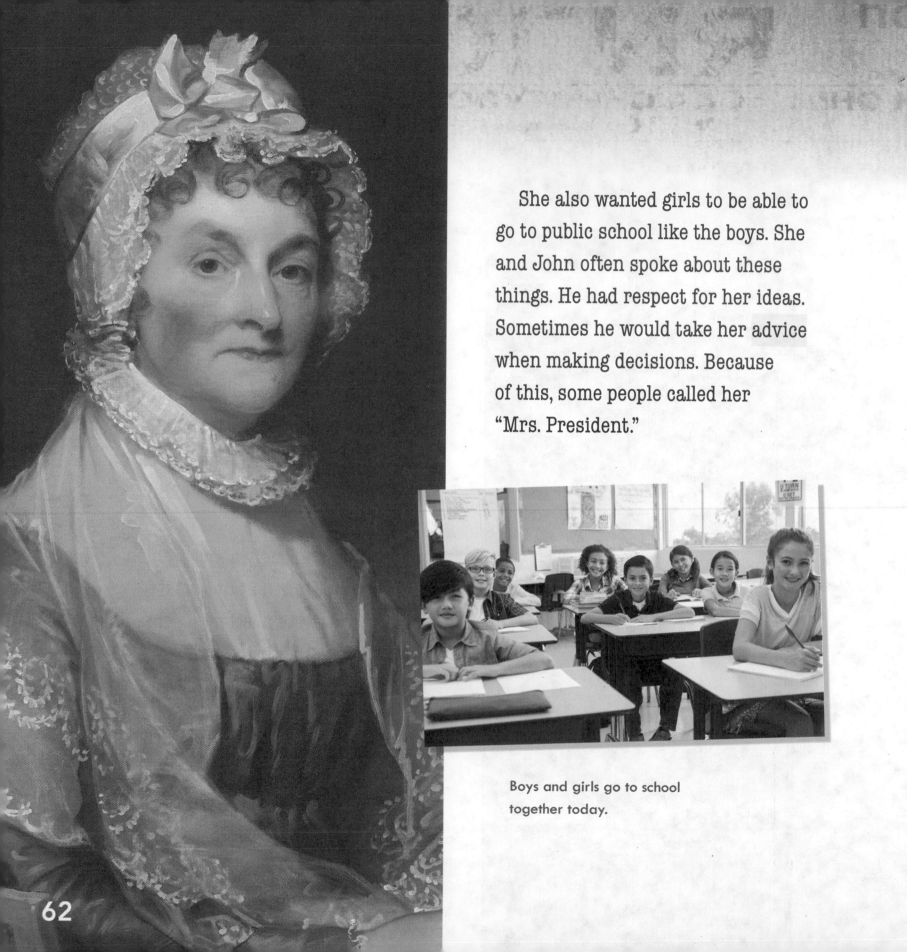

She also wanted girls to be able to go to public school like the boys. She and John often spoke about these things. He had respect for her ideas. Sometimes he would take her advice when making decisions. Because of this, some people called her "Mrs. President."

Boys and girls go to school together today.

As you can see, Abigail Adams did things that were unusual for women in her time. She helped her husband make decisions for the country. She talked about rights for women. She did jobs around the house that were usually done by men. Because of these reasons, I think Abigail Adams was a great example of a leader!

Statue of Abigail Adams in Boston

63

Hi! I'm Anthony!

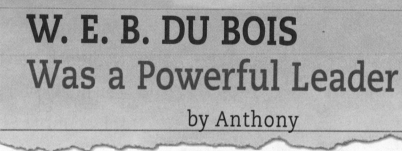

W. E. B. Du Bois

W. E. B. DU BOIS
Was a Powerful Leader
by Anthony

I think W. E. B. Du Bois was an important leader in our country. He worked to change what he did not like. He wanted to help others, and he did. He also earned the respect of people around the world.

Harvard University

In 1895, W. E. B. Du Bois graduated from Harvard University, one of the best colleges in our country. He was the first African American to earn a special degree from there called a Ph.D. He led the way for others who wanted an education. While most people spend four years in college, W. E. B. Du Bois chose to stay longer. This shows he was a hard worker.

W. E. B. Du Bois had many jobs throughout his life. One of those jobs was a teacher. In a way, teachers are leaders. They set examples for how their students should act.

W. E. B. Du Bois

W. E. B. Du Bois felt strongly about people's rights. When he moved to Tennessee, he found that some people did not have the same rights as others. This made him sad and angry. He tried to fix the problem. W. E. B. Du Bois wrote papers and gave speeches about equal rights. He became a famous supporter of equal rights. Being active in the community made W. E. B. Du Bois a better leader. He knew how to reach people.

Mural of W. E. B. Du Bois
in Philadelphia

W. E. B. Du Bois expected a lot from
himself and others. He was a good role
model who showed others how to make
positive changes. I think we should
learn from his actions. If we do, we can
all be leaders! Don't you agree?

Great Leaders

Use details from *Great Leaders* to answer these questions with a partner.

1. **Evaluate** What are the most important details to remember about Abigail Adams and W. E. B. Du Bois? Look for clues in the text and pictures to help you decide.

2. Find two facts and two opinions about Abigail Adams. Then find two facts and two opinions about W. E. B. Du Bois. How do the opinions help you get to know the authors?

3. Why did the authors write these texts? What do they want to persuade you to think?

Talking Tip

Use your own words to explain details from the text. Complete the sentence below.

I read that _____ .

Write an Opinion

PROMPT Both Abigail Adams and W. E. B. Du Bois worked to make changes. How do you think their actions changed the lives of others? Use details from the words and photos to explain your ideas.

PLAN First, list the things that were important to Abigail Adams and W. E. B. Du Bois. Think about who they wanted to help.

Abigail Adams	W. E. B. Du Bois

WRITE Now write an opinion that explains how you think their actions changed the lives of others. Remember to:

- Use opinion words like *I think* or *I believe*.

- Use examples from their lives to support your ideas.

_____

_____

_____

_____

_____

_____

_____

_____

_____

_____

Prepare to Read

GENRE STUDY **Opinion writing** shows an author's thoughts, beliefs, or ideas.

MAKE A PREDICTION Preview "Kids for President!" The author thinks kids should run for president. How do you think the author will get readers to agree with him?

_____

_____

_____

_____

_____

_____

SET A PURPOSE Read to find out why the author thinks kids would make good presidents.

Kids for President!

READ Which details show an opinion? <u>Underline</u> them.

Would you like to be president when you grow up? Why wait? In my opinion, kids like us would make great presidents. A president has to be fair when he or she is making decisions. Kids learn about being fair all the time. A president has to work well with other world leaders. Kids are experts at taking turns. We know how to share and follow rules, too. ▶

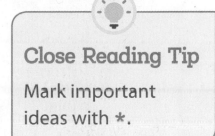

Close Reading Tip

Mark important ideas with *.

CHECK MY UNDERSTANDING

What is the author's opinion about who can be president? What reasons does he give to support it?

_____

_____

_____

READ The author includes facts and opinions. <u>Underline</u> a sentence that tells a fact.

Close Reading Tip

Mark important ideas with *.

A president has to be a good listener. He or she needs to hear what is important to people. That helps the president make good decisions. Kids are great listeners. Kids listen to their parents, their teachers, and their friends every day.

Kids are good at dreaming, too. We have big imaginations. That would be a very helpful thing for a president. If a president thinks big, amazing things can happen for everyone in the country.

That's why I think kids should be president.

CHECK MY UNDERSTANDING

Which details help you decide if a kid can be president?

_____

_____

_____

_____

WRITE ABOUT IT The author of "Kids for President!" thinks kids would make good presidents. Do you agree or disagree? Use details from the text to explain your opinion.

_____

_____

_____

_____

_____

_____

_____

_____

_____

_____

_____

Prepare to Read

GENRE STUDY **Informational text** is nonfiction. It gives facts about a topic. As you read *Who Are Government's Leaders?*, look for:

- captions with photos
- main topic and details
- headings that stand out

SET A PURPOSE As you read, **summarize** the text. Use your own words to describe the most important ideas in an order that makes sense.

POWER WORDS

troop

charge

solve

state

members

laws

capital

council

Build Background: What Is Government?

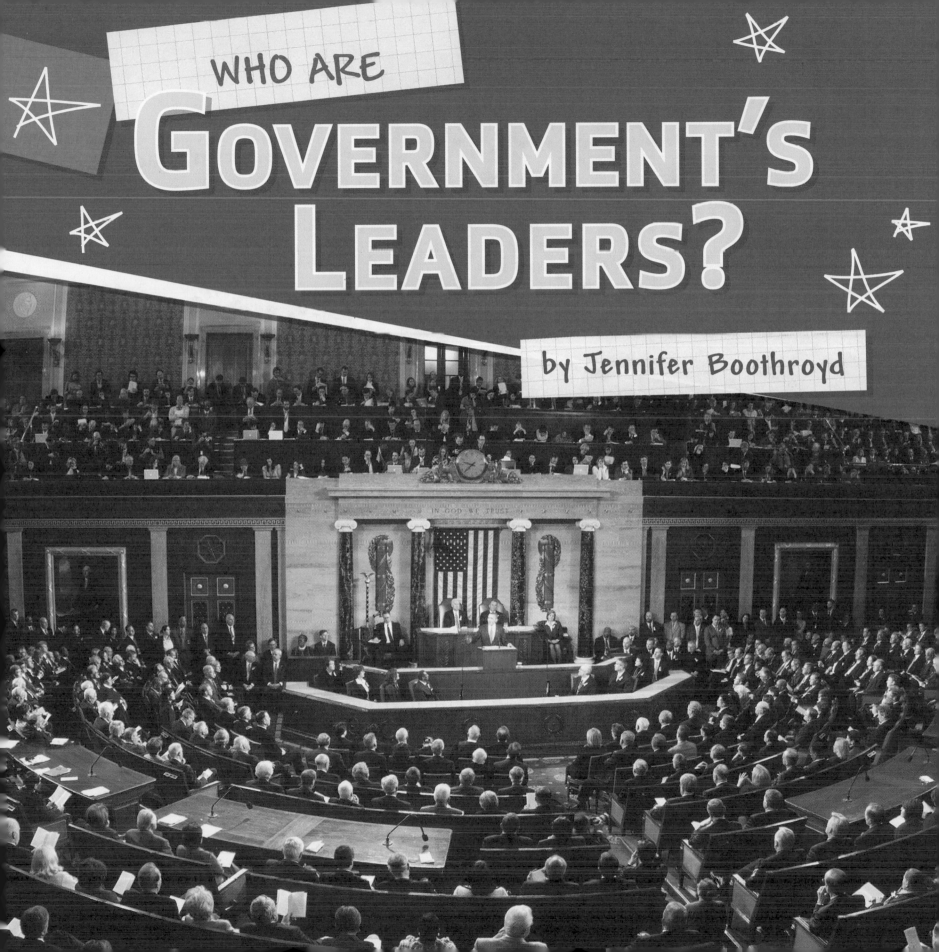

WHO ARE GOVERNMENT'S LEADERS?

by Jennifer Boothroyd

Government leaders write rules for us to follow.

This leader helps guide the scouts in his troop.

Who Is a Leader?

A leader is a person who is in charge of a group of people. Leaders try to help their groups and solve problems. Leaders try to work together and are good listeners, too.

Some leaders work in government. Government leaders help make rules. They make rules for our country, our state, and our city.

Our Country's Leaders

Our country's leaders work in Washington, D.C. The president leads our country, and **members** of Congress make **laws** for our country. The president and Congress work together.

Capitol Building in Washington, D.C.

Most governors are chosen every four years.

⭐ State Leaders

State leaders work in the state's capital city. People in each state choose a governor. The governor leads the state. The governor works with legislators, who make laws for their state.

 # City Leaders

A mayor is the leader of a city's government. The mayor works with the city council.

Citizens choose council members.

Good leaders make our country a
better place to live.

Turn and Talk

Use details from *Who Are Government's Leaders?* to answer these questions with a partner.

1. **Summarize** What did you learn about government leaders from reading this text?

2. Why is being a good listener an important part of being a government leader?

3. What do you think is the most interesting part of being a government leader? What do you think is the most difficult part?

Listening Tip

Look at your partner as you listen. Nod your head to show you are interested.

Write a Help Wanted Ad

PROMPT A help wanted ad is an advertisement that appears in a newspaper when a job needs to be filled. It tells people what it takes to do that job. What would you write in a help wanted ad for a government leader? Use details from the words and photos to explain your ideas.

PLAN First, think about the skills that good government leaders need to have. Add them to the web.

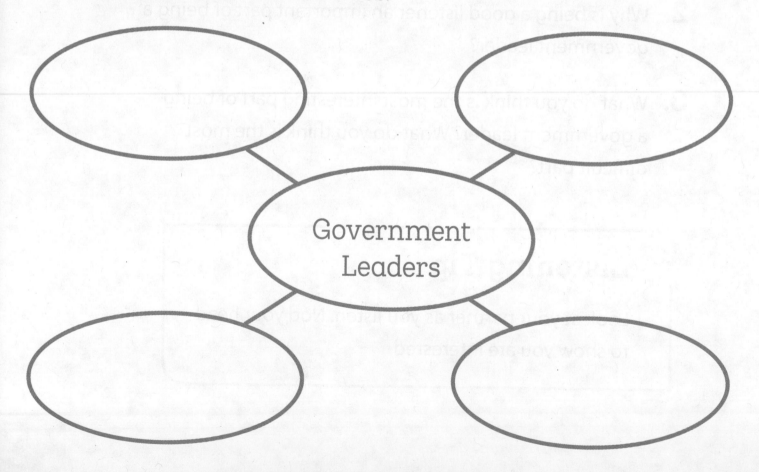

Government Leaders

WRITE Now write a help wanted ad for a job as a government leader. Remember to:

- Describe the skills a person will need to do a good job.

- Explain why this job is important.

_____

_____

_____

_____

_____

_____

_____

_____

_____

_____

_____

Prepare to Read

GENRE STUDY **Informational text** is nonfiction. It gives facts about a topic.

MAKE A PREDICTION Preview "Learn First! Then Vote!" Voting for good leaders is very important. What do you think this text will be about?

_____

_____

_____

_____

_____

_____

SET A PURPOSE Read to find out about how people choose who will get their vote.

Learn First! Then Vote!

READ What is a candidate? <u>Underline</u> the sentence that helps you understand the word's meaning.

In the United States, citizens vote for government leaders. Being a government leader is a very important job. People count on them to make careful decisions. Choosing who to vote for is a very important job, too. How do people decide who will get their vote? Let's find out!

First, people think about the issues that are important to them. Building good schools is one example of an important issue. Then people learn about each candidate, or person who is running for office. They ask, "How does each candidate feel about the issues I care about most?"

> **Close Reading Tip**
> Circle words you don't know. Then figure them out.

READ What are some ways to learn about a candidate?

There are many ways to learn about candidates. One way is to watch a debate. A debate is a discussion between people who disagree. When candidates debate, they share their opinions about issues.

Another way to learn is to read. During an election, newspapers have stories about candidates. People write books about them, too. Some candidates even write their own books.

When it is time to vote, people think about all they have learned. Then they ask, "Who do I think will do the best job?" Then they make their choice.

CHECK MY UNDERSTANDING

What are the most important ideas on this page?

_____

_____

_____

_____

WRITE ABOUT IT In your own words, tell what you learned. Write a summary of "Learn First! Then Vote!"

_____

_____

_____

_____

_____

_____

_____

_____

_____

_____

_____

_____

_____

Prepare to View

GENRE STUDY **Videos** are short movies that give you information or something for you to watch for enjoyment. As you watch *Thomas Edison and the Light Bulb*, notice:

- how pictures, sounds, and words work together
- what the video is about
- information about the topic
- the tone or mood of the video

SET A PURPOSE One way to tell events is in **chronological order.** That means they are told in the order they happened. Pay attention to the order of events in the video. How does the order help you understand how the events are related?

Build Background: What Inventors Do

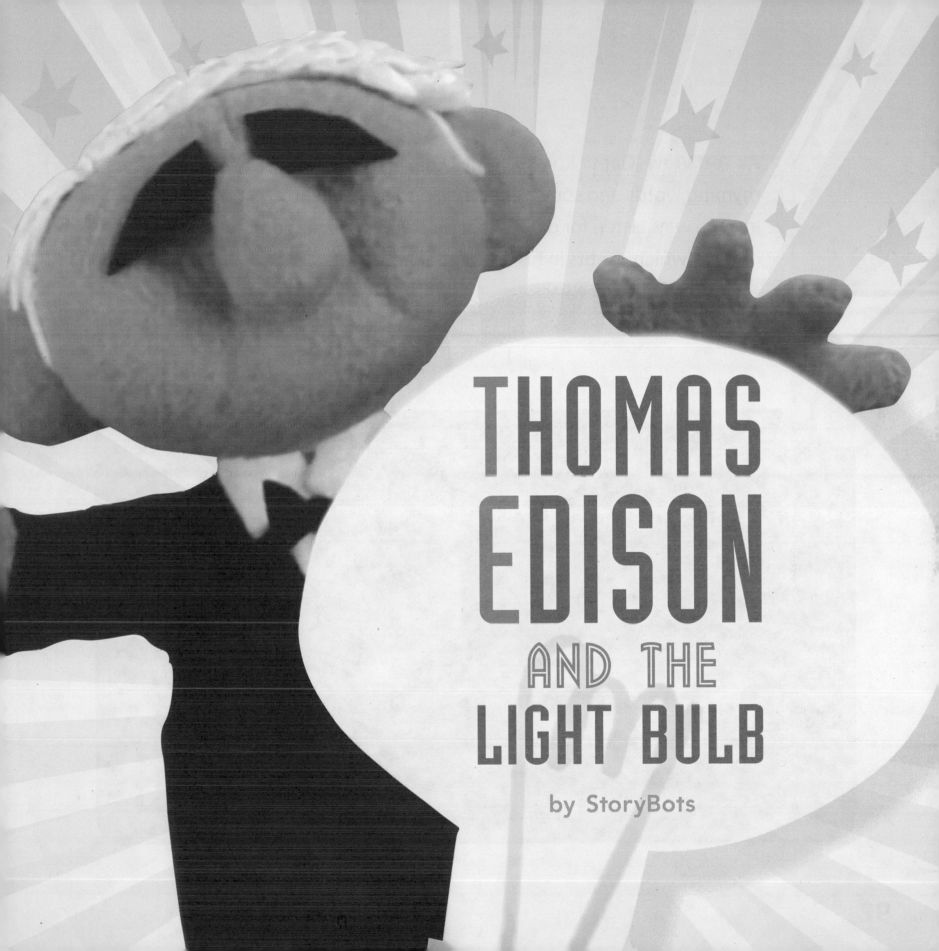

THOMAS EDISON
AND THE LIGHT BULB

by StoryBots

As You View Get to know Thomas Edison! Think about how rhyming words and sound effects help to tell Mr. Edison's story in a fun way. Listen for details that help you understand the order in which events in his life happened.

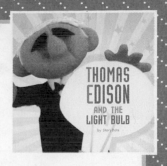

Turn and Talk

Use details from *Thomas Edison and the Light Bulb* to answer these questions with a partner.

1. Chronological Order What was the order of events that led to Edison's invention of the light bulb?

2. Why does the video show Edison throwing a plant onto a giant pile of plants? How does that help you understand how Edison felt about inventing?

3. What do Thomas Edison and Maya In *Going Places* have in common? What makes them both leaders?

Talking Tip

Ask to learn more about one of your partner's ideas. Complete the sentence below.

Please explain _____.

Let's Wrap Up!

? **Essential Question**

What are the qualities of a good leader?

Pick one of these activities to show what you have learned about the topic.

1. Interview a Leader

Think about the different leaders you read about in the texts. Which one would you most like to meet? Write five questions you would like to ask if you could interview that person.

Word Challenge

Can you use the word inspire in one of your questions?

2. Getting to Know Leaders

With a group, role-play a conversation between the leaders you read about. Have each group member be a different leader. Take turns introducing yourselves and describing what makes you a leader. Use details from the texts to explain your ideas.

My Notes

Weather Wise

"We'll weather the weather, whatever
the weather, whether we like it or not."

—Anonymous

? Essential Question

How does weather affect us?

Get Curious Video

Words About Weather

Complete the Vocabulary Network to show what you know about the words.

climate	
Meaning: **Climate** is the normal weather of a place.	
Synonyms and Antonyms	Drawing

precipitation

Meaning: **Precipitation** is water that falls from the sky, such as rain, sleet, hail, or snow.

Synonyms and Antonyms	Drawing

temperature

Meaning: **Temperature** is how hot or cold a place is.

Synonyms and Antonyms	Drawing

WEATHER THROUGH THE SEASONS

Weather is what the air is like outside. A weather map shows the weather in different places. Weather maps use symbols, shapes, and colors. Together, these things show us what the weather will be like.

Average Summer Temperature

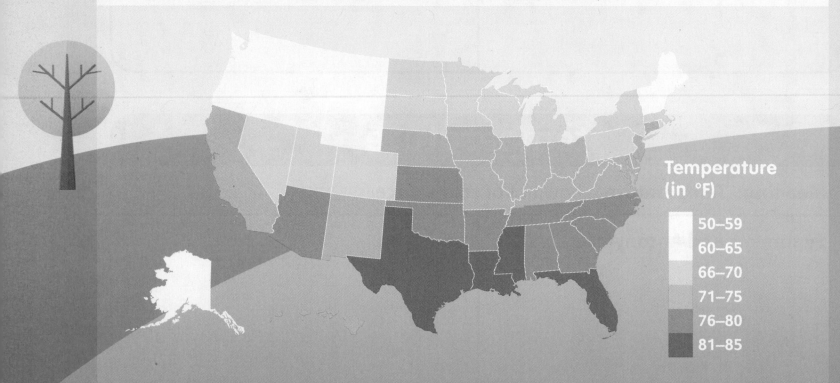

Temperature (in °F)

50–59
60–65
66–70
71–75
76–80
81–85

What does the map show you about summer weather in different parts of the country?

What do the words and pictures below tell you about winter weather?

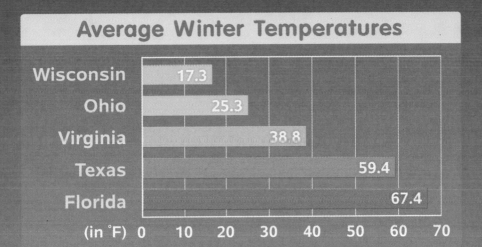

Average Winter Temperatures

State	Temperature (in °F)
Wisconsin	17.3
Ohio	25.3
Virginia	38.8
Texas	59.4
Florida	67.4

(in °F) 0 10 20 30 40 50 60 70

Average Yearly Snowfall

Inches of Snow

- 50 or more
- 25 to 50
- 12 to 25
- 1 to 12
- 0 to 1

How do summer and winter in your state compare to other parts of the country?

Prepare to Read

GENRE STUDY **Narrative nonfiction** gives facts about a topic, but it reads like a story. As you read *Wild Weather,* look for:

- information and facts about a real topic
- visuals such as maps or diagrams with text
- ways that visuals and words help readers understand the text

SET A PURPOSE Read to make smart guesses, or **inferences,** about things the author does not say. Use clues in the text and pictures to help you.

POWER WORDS

tough

pellets

predict

clings

funnel

occur

excess

damage

Meet Thomas Kingsley Troupe.

WILD WEATHER

by Thomas Kingsley Troupe

illustrated by Jamey Christoph

High up, along a mountain trail,
a hiker sat and folded an origami bird.

"It sure is sunny," she said. As she
held the bird high, a gust of wind lifted
the paper. The bird began to fly.

"Whoa, how did
it get so windy?"

Just then, the bird spotted
a duck flying nearby.

"Hey, there.
What's your name?"

The bird remembered
the hiker had said *sunny*.

"Sonny, I think."

"I'm Chuck. Nice to meet
you, Sonny. Say, I've got a real
problem. My wife, Natasha, is
missing. We were trying to fly
away from here."

"Why do you want to leave?" Sonny asked.
The mountain valley looked nice enough.

"Aren't you a bird? Most birds
fly south before winter. This wind
is making flying tough!"

"Where did all this
wind come from?"

WARM AIR

COOL AIR

"It's simple," he said. "The sun heats the land, making the air above it warm. The warm air rises. Cool air rushes to take the place of the warm air. And because Earth spins, wind can come from any direction."

"So, do you think the wind carried Natasha away?" Sonny asked.

"I hope not," Chuck cried. "She was right next to me, but then she disappeared!"

A drop of water struck Sonny's wing.

"Just what we need! It's raining! Fly underneath me, Sonny. I don't think wet paper is good for flying."

"Clouds and rain? How did they get here?"

"Check out this water cycle chart. It explains how clouds form and rain falls."

"Wow! That's pretty simple, really."

WATER CYCLE

The sun heats water on the ground, turning it into an invisible gas.

Gas rises, cools, and turns into water droplets.

Water droplets clump together to form clouds.

Water droplets combine and fall as rain.

"So rain is just a bunch of tiny droplets?" Sonny said. "That doesn't seem so bad."

"Normal rainstorms are fine. But thunderstorms can make lightning and heavy rain. When too much rain falls all at once, a flood can form."

"Whoa!"

"Hang on," Chuck yelled. "Hail is falling!"

"Hail?" Sonny chirped. "What's that?"

"Sometimes storm clouds called cumulonimbus clouds form. Water droplets in the highest parts of the cloud bounce around and freeze into ice pellets," Chuck said. "The pellets hit water droplets, and the hail gets bigger."

"And once the hail is too heavy, it falls?" Sonny asked.

"You got it," Chuck shouted. "Come on, let's head for the woods!"

"Isn't there any way to know when the weather will get wild?"

"There is! Meteorologists study and predict weather. They use tools to help them."

"Weather tools?" Sonny asked. "Like what?"

"They have instruments to measure wind speed and direction," Chuck explained. "And radar to track rain and thunderstorms. Meteorologists even use satellites in outer space to track how and where the clouds move."

Sonny shivered. His papery body was growing cold.

"Natasha is lost, and it will snow any day now." Chuck quacked sadly.

"So what's the deal with snow?"

"It's a bit different than hail. The water vapor turns into an ice crystal. The ice crystal clings to other crystals and forms a snowflake."

"That doesn't sound so bad," Sonny said.

"If the ground and air are cold enough, the snowflakes pile up and cover the ground," Chuck quacked. "The lakes freeze, and it's tough for birds like us to find food."

"Oh! So that's why you fly south!"

"I'm not flying south without my wife! Natasha!" Chuck quacked. "Where are you?"

"How's the weather down south?"

"It's much warmer. But the weather can get wild there too."

"What do you mean?" Sonny asked.

"Heat is measured in temperature," Chuck explained. "When the air is hot, the temperature is high. A low temperature means it's cool."

"That makes sense," Sonny said.

"Too much heat can hurt people, plants . . . even animals," Chuck quacked. "During a heat wave, the temperature and humidity stay high for two or more days."

"I wouldn't want to be stuck in one of those!" Sonny said.

Where was the worst heat wave on record? That would be 'down under.' The temperature in Marble Bar, Australia, was over 100 degrees Fahrenheit (38 degrees Celsius) for 160 days in a row in 1923. Hot days, mate!

"Where is Natasha? She couldn't have just disappeared!"

"What happened to those trees?"

"A tornado came through here years ago," Chuck said.

"What's a tornado?" Sonny asked.

"It's a funnel of wind that forms in the sky and wrecks what it touches on the ground," Chuck said. "Tornadoes form during a thunderstorm. They are more likely to occur over flat land."

"But how?" Sonny asked.

"When the wind in a storm changes direction, increases speed, and rises, it makes the air below it spin. Rising air pushes the spinning column of air downward until it's vertical. The spinning funnel of air speeds up, forming a tornado."

Tornadoes are usually determined to be weak, strong, or violent. The violent ones can have winds in excess of 200 miles (322 kilometers) per hour. They can destroy homes. Only 2 percent of tornadoes are violent.

"I had no idea weather could be so scary," Sonny said.

"That's nothing. My cousin Frank almost got caught in a hurricane once."

"A hurricane? I'm afraid to ask!"

"A hurricane forms in summer or fall," Chuck said. "It forms over an ocean and moves toward land."

"Does it make lots of wind like a tornado?" asked Sonny.

"Yes. Strong winds rotate around the 'eye' of the storm," said Chuck. "The spinning storm picks up energy from the warmth of the ocean. When it hits land, high winds and heavy rain can damage buildings."

The "eye" of a hurricane is the spot in the center of the storm. In the eye, the winds are light or calm, clouds break up and rain ends as the sky clears.

"Wow, all that dangerous weather scares me!" said Sonny.

"Here's the thing, Sonny," Chuck said. "We can't control weather. But meteorologists can warn everyone when dangerous weather is coming, and we can prepare for it."

"Hey, Chuck. Is that your wife?"

"It is! Where were you, Natasha?"

"I went back for my sunglasses. I can't fly south without them!"

"Come with us, Sonny," Chuck said.

"I'd love to!" Sonny said. "But can I get some of those cool Sonny-glasses too?"

Turn and Talk

Use details from *Wild Weather* to answer these questions with a partner.

1. **Make Inferences** Why is a meteorologist's job important?

2. Look at the chart on page 109. How can you use the text and pictures to find and understand information about the water cycle?

3. In what ways is a hurricane like a tornado? How are they different? Use details from the text and pictures to explain your answer.

Talking Tip

Speak clearly as you share your ideas. Do not speak too quickly or too slowly.

I think that _____.

Write an Opinion

PROMPT When you recommend a book, you try to persuade someone else to read it. What would you say to recommend *Wild Weather*? Think about what you liked best about the text and illustrations.

PLAN First, write three reasons you would give to persuade someone to read *Wild Weather*.

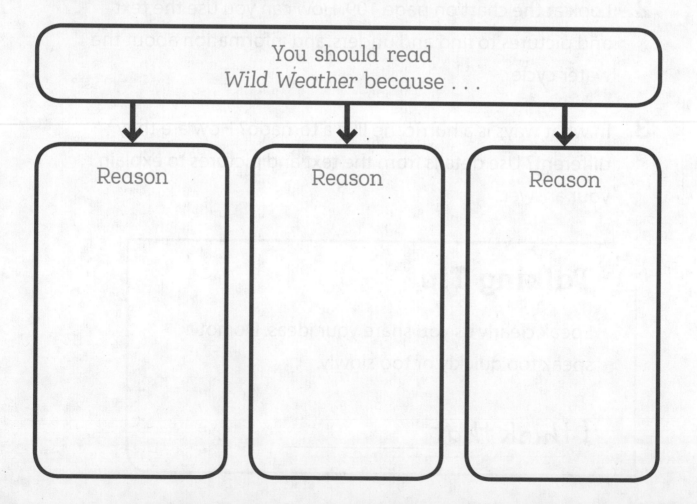

You should read
Wild Weather because . . .

Reason

Reason

Reason

WRITE Now write your opinion. Tell why you would recommend *Wild Weather*. Remember to:

- Use details that tell what readers will learn from *Wild Weather*.
- Use language that will make readers excited about reading it!

_____

_____

_____

_____

_____

_____

_____

_____

_____

_____

_____

_____

Prepare to Read

GENRE STUDY > **Narrative nonfiction** gives facts about a topic, but it reads like a story.

MAKE A PREDICTION > Preview "North for the Winter." Two ducks decide not to fly south for the winter. What do you think will happen that winter?

_____

_____

_____

_____

_____

_____

SET A PURPOSE > Read to find out what the ducks learn about what it's like during winter.

North for the Winter

READ Why do Hank and Diego stay up north? <u>Underline</u> the sentence that tells you.

In fall, it begins to get cool up north. Ducks fly south to where it is warm. All the ducks except Hank and Diego, that is.

"Every year, the leaves turn brown and the ducks leave town," said Diego. "This year, I want to see what winter's all about. I am going to stay right here and see my first winter."

"Me, too!" Hank said, excitedly. "I want to see snow!" ▶

Close Reading Tip

Mark important ideas with *.

CHECK MY UNDERSTANDING

Why do ducks fly south in winter? Why is Hank excited to stay?

_____

_____

_____

Close Reading Tip

<u>Underline</u> two facts that Hank and Diego learn about winter.

READ What causes ice to form in winter?

In winter, the days are shorter and the temperatures are colder than in any other time of year. Water turns to ice because temperatures fall below freezing. Snow may fall, too.

"*Brrr*," Hank said. "It sure is chilly here in winter."

"Did you see what happened to our duck pond?" Diego asked. "The water turned to a solid, and it's super slippery."

Hank and Diego had fun sliding on their frozen pond. Suddenly, a snowflake fell. Soon many snowflakes were falling.

"Woo-hoo!" shouted Hank. "Time to make snowducks!"

"Hooray!" Diego cheered. "After that, let's head south to warm up. I can't wait to tell everyone about our snowducks!"

CHECK MY UNDERSTANDING

Which clue word helps you figure out why ice forms in winter?

_____

_____

_____

WRITE ABOUT IT Write a letter from Hank and Diego to their friends in the south to tell what winter is like and what they have learned. Use details from the text in your letter.

_____

_____

_____

_____

_____

_____

_____

_____

_____

_____

Prepare to Read

GENRE STUDY **Fantasies** are stories with made-up events that could not really happen. As you read *Cloudette,* look for:

- characters that are not found in real life
- a lesson the main character learns
- problems and solutions

SET A PURPOSE As you read, **make connections** by finding ways that this text is like things in your life and other texts you have read. This will help you understand and remember the text.

POWER WORDS

average

advantages

front

impressed

Meet Tom Lichtenheld.

Cloudette

by Tom Lichtenheld

Cloudette was a cloud.
A very small cloud.

Usually, Cloudette didn't mind being smaller than the average cloud.

Cloudette

Average Cloud

In fact, being small had lots of advantages.

Morning, small-fry.

Hey, shortcake!

Hi, pipsqueak!

Everyone called her cute little names.

She had lots of little friends.

No matter how crowded it was, she could always find a good spot to watch fireworks.

She could sneak through tight spaces,

hide in small places,

and she even had a special little space
that always made her feel cozy at night.

But once in a while, all the other clouds would run off to do something big and important.

135

Cloudette could see them in the distance, doing
all sorts of important cloud things.

This made her want to do big and important things, too.

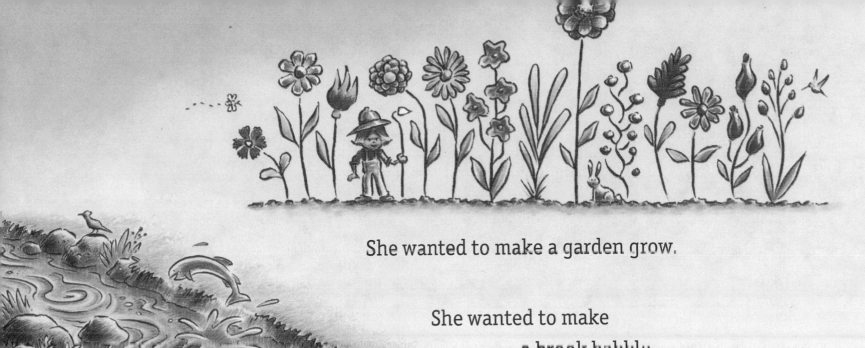

She wanted to make a garden grow.

She wanted to make
a brook babble.

She

wanted

to

make

a

waterfall

fall.

And she thought nothing
would be more fun than giving
some kids a day off from school.

137

One night, Cloudette lay awake wondering
what she could do that was big and important.

She thought maybe she could work
for the fire department.

Sorry, we just got a
brand-new pumper truck.

Or maybe they needed some help
down at the garden center.

Sorry, these plants
take TONS of water.

But nobody seemed
to need her.

Sorry, it's all
done by machines.

Cloudette was feeling blue.

The next day, there was a big storm in Cloudette's neighborhood.

The sky got dark, the rain came down like cats and dogs, and the wind blew harder than she'd ever seen wind blow before.

When the storm finally stopped, Cloudette realized she'd been blown far from her neighborhood.

She didn't know anyone here.

Hello.
Hi.
Howdy.
Howya doin'?

And they didn't seem eager to get to know her.

But pretty soon she was making new friends and seeing things she'd never seen before.

Then she heard something she'd never heard before.

ribbit

She looked down at what was supposed to be a pond,
but was really just a puddle of mud.

What happened to your pond, froggie?

*It dried up, and now it's more
like a puddle than a pond.*

This gave Cloudette an idea . . .

*More like a
brainstorm,
actually.*

144

She held her breath until she
started to puff up all over.

Then she turned a
nice blue-gray color.

She kept growing until
it looked like she was
ready to burst.

She shook her behind until it made a little
rumbling sound—not quite what you'd call
thunder, but enough to let people know they
might want to grab an umbrella.

Then she did what she'd wanted to do for ages.

She

let

it

pour.

Cloudette rained on
that little puddle until it
grew into a big puddle.

And she kept on raining
until that big puddle

grew into a perfect pond.

As soon as she stopped, frogs of every stripe
(and spot) came jumping into the pond.

They all let out a big "Thank you!" in unison.

Cloudette was exhausted, but happy.

* "Thank you!" in Frog

Nice work, cloudy.

Yeah, way to water!

Prodigious precipitation, pipsqueak!

That was some righteous rain!

We knew you had it in you!

Even the higher-ups were impressed, which got her thinking . . .

149

*I'll bet there are other
big and important things
a little cloud can do.*

And off she went.

Turn and Talk

Cloudette
by Tom Lichtenheld

Use details from *Cloudette* to answer these questions with a partner.

1. Make Connections Think about a time when you were not big enough to do something you really wanted to do. How does that help you understand Cloudette's feelings?

2. How do the other characters in the story feel about Cloudette? What does this tell you about what she is like? Use details from the text and illustrations to explain your answer.

3. What does Cloudette learn about herself?

Listening Tip

Listen carefully. Make connections. How is what your partner is saying like other things you know?

Write the Next Chapter

PROMPT What will Cloudette do next? Use what you know about her to write about her next adventure. Look for details in the words and pictures to help you think of ideas.

PLAN First, draw a picture that shows what you think Cloudette will do next. Add a caption to describe what she is doing.

WRITE Now write a new adventure for Cloudette! Remember to:

- Look for details in the story that give clues about what Cloudette likes to do.
- Include details that describe what Cloudette is seeing, thinking, and feeling.

_____

_____

_____

_____

_____

_____

_____

_____

_____

_____

Prepare to Read

GENRE STUDY **Fantasies** are stories with made-up events that could not really happen.

MAKE A PREDICTION Preview "Raining Cats and Dogs!" Misty wants to play in the rain. You know that most stories include a problem. What problem do you think Misty will have?

_____

_____

_____

_____

_____

_____

SET A PURPOSE Read to find out about Misty's rainy day and to find out if your prediction is correct. If not, use what you know about story structure to make a new prediction.

Raining Cats and Dogs!

READ Is the narrator a character in the story? How can you tell?

One rainy morning, Misty brought her leash to her owner, Annie. Misty was still a pup, and she loved to splash in the puddles. She wagged her tail and barked happily to let Annie know it was time for them to go out. Annie grinned.

"We can't take our walk yet, Misty," Annie said, pointing out the window. "It's raining cats and dogs out there!"

Shocked, Misty dashed to the window and looked out eagerly. She had never seen it rain cats and dogs before. It sounded amazing! To her surprise, Misty just saw an ordinary rainy day. She watched the raindrops fall and wondered where the cats and dogs were. ▶

Close Reading Tip

Underline the problem.

READ What does Misty do to solve her problem? <u>Underline</u> it.

Close Reading Tip

Write C when you make a connection to something in your life.

Later, the sky cleared and the sun came out. Finally, Annie took Misty for a walk. They even went to the dog park, Misty's favorite place to meet her friends. At the dog park, Misty saw Dash, the next-door neighbor's dog.

Dash was older and wiser, so Misty asked, "Why did Annie tell me it was raining cats and dogs this morning? There wasn't a dog or cat in sight. What was she talking about?"

Dash laughed and explained, "That is just something humans like to say. It means it is raining very hard and they don't want to go for a walk. It makes no sense, but we have to be patient with our humans. They can be so silly sometimes."

CHECK MY UNDERSTANDING

What does "raining cats and dogs" mean?

_____

_____

_____

WRITE ABOUT IT Write a journal entry to describe the day from Misty's point of view. Be sure to tell the events in order.

_____

_____

_____

_____

_____

_____

_____

_____

_____

_____

_____

Prepare to Read

GENRE STUDY **Informational text** is nonfiction. It gives facts about a topic. As you read *Get Ready for Weather*, look for:

- captions with art or photos
- headings, subheadings, or bold words that stand out
- how visuals and words help you understand the text

SET A PURPOSE Think carefully about the author's words as you read. Then **evaluate,** or decide, which details are most important to help you understand the text.

POWER WORDS

gusts

flash

supplies

layer

Build Background: What a Meteorologist Does

GET READY FOR WEATHER

by Lucy Jones

What's the Weather?

Take a look outside your window. What's the weather like today? It might be sunny or cloudy, rainy or snowy. One of the neat things about weather is that it's always changing. Temperatures can be warm or cold. Winds can be strong gusts or soft breezes. If it's rainy and chilly today, it could be sunny and warm tomorrow.

Meteorologists tell us the weather.

People check the weather forecast to help plan their days. It tells if the weather will be rainy or sunny, hot or cold. Knowing what the weather will be helps people decide what to wear and do each day. If a big storm is on the way, the forecast explains what to expect and how to prepare.

Today's Forecast: Thunderstorms

Thunderstorms are storms that have rain, thunder, and lightning. Lightning can be very dangerous. Lightning can strike trees and telephone poles. The bright flash of lightning can be seen from very far away. Sometimes it can be seen from 100 miles away!

Thunderstorms usually happen in spring and summer.

162

If you hear the rumble of thunder, it is a good idea to <u>go inside right away.</u> Indoors is the best place to be during a thunderstorm. If you are outdoors, keep low to the ground. Also, be sure to stay away from trees.

Try This!

You can figure out how far lightning is from you! If you see lightning, start counting seconds until you hear thunder. For every 5 seconds you count, that's one mile away!

Today's Forecast: Blizzard

Blizzards are winter storms. They have very heavy snow and strong winds. It is hard to see in a blizzard. It can also be hard to walk because of the wind and the deep snow.

Blizzard Shopping

Stores get very crowded before a blizzard. People buy batteries and flashlights in case the electricity goes out. They buy extra food and water, too. Having the right **supplies** is one way to prepare for a storm.

After a blizzard, there is LOTS of shoveling to do! Snowplows work day and night to clear the roads. Neighbors help each other shovel sidewalks and driveways. School might be canceled for a few days. Kids can go sledding and build snowmen, but they better bundle up first! Wearing more than one layer of clothes will keep them warm in the frosty cold.

Today's Forecast: Sandstorm

Sandstorms happen when strong winds pick up sand. In the air, the sand forms into cloud shapes. In very strong winds, these sand clouds can grow to be 50 feet high! The winds can carry the sand for many miles. Sandstorms usually happen in dry, hot areas.

Sandstorms can form very quickly.

The best place to be during a sandstorm is indoors with the windows shut.

Being outside during a sandstorm is unsafe. Imagine being inside a swirling cloud of sand. It would be <u>very hard</u> to see. Sand could get in your eyes, nose, ears, and mouth. Covering your face with a cloth and wearing glasses is one way to protect yourself. Finding shelter and staying there until the storm is over is another way to stay safe.

Meteorologists use tools to help predict when and where storms will arrive. Knowing that a storm is coming can help you prepare. Storms can be dangerous, but they can be beautiful, too. Stay safe and enjoy the weather wherever you live!

Sometimes a rainbow appears after a rainstorm.

Keeping Pets Safe

When a big storm hits, pets need to be protected, too. Be sure your pets are indoors with you where it is safe and warm!

Use details from *Get Ready for Weather* to answer these questions with a partner.

1. **Evaluate** Which details in *Get Ready for Weather* help you understand how to get ready for a blizzard?

2. Look back at pages 162–163. What is the main idea of this section? What details tell more about it?

3. Compare *Get Ready for Weather* and *Wild Weather*. How are the texts alike? What are the most important differences between them?

Talking Tip

Complete the sentence to add to what your partner says.

My idea is _____.

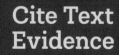

Write Safety Tips

PROMPT What can you do to stay safe during different kinds of weather? Use details from the words and pictures in *Get Ready for Weather* to explain your ideas.

PLAN First, list some ways to stay safe during thunderstorms, blizzards, and sandstorms.

Thunderstorm	Blizzard	Sandstorm

WRITE Now write five safety tips that will help people and pets stay safe during different kinds of weather. Remember to:

- Use verbs that tell people exactly what to do.
- Number each of your safety tips.

_____

_____

_____

_____

_____

_____

_____

_____

_____

_____

Prepare to Read

GENRE STUDY **Informational text** is nonfiction. It gives facts about a topic.

MAKE A PREDICTION Preview "Protect Yourself." Read the title and the headings. What do you think the text will be about?

_____

_____

_____

_____

_____

_____

_____

SET A PURPOSE Read to learn facts and to see if your prediction is right. If not, think about what you've read in the text and what the title and headings tell you. Then make a new prediction.

Protect Yourself

READ How does the picture help you understand the text?

There are many ways to enjoy different kinds of weather, but it's important to be prepared before you step outside.

Clothing

In cold weather, bundle up in coats, hats, mittens, earmuffs, and scarves to keep your body warm. In very hot weather, wear lighter clothes like shorts and t-shirts. When it's raining, wear a raincoat and rain boots to keep you dry.

Close Reading Tip

Underline the central idea.

CHECK MY UNDERSTANDING

What are two ways clothing can protect you from weather?

_____

_____

READ What safety details are important to know for hot weather? <u>Underline</u> them.

Close Reading Tip

Mark important ideas with *.

Follow Safety Tips

On sunny days, wearing sunscreen and sunglasses will help protect your skin and eyes. Sunny days can be hot or cold.

Drinking lots of water on a hot, sunny day is important. Your body loses water when it's hot. Keeping all parts of your body covered in very cold weather will help protect your skin.

Knowing the weather forecast helps keep you safe, too.

Don't go outside when there is a thunderstorm on the way. Be sure to take breaks from being outside when it is very hot or very cold, too. Enjoy the outdoors safely!

CHECK MY UNDERSTANDING

How do the headings help you understand what you are reading?

_____

_____

_____

WRITE ABOUT IT Choose one type of weather and write a paragraph explaining how to protect yourself from that kind of weather. Include information you learned from the text.

_____

_____

_____

_____

_____

_____

_____

_____

_____

_____

Prepare to Read

GENRE STUDY   **Poetry** uses images, sounds, and rhythm to express feelings. As you read the poems in *Whatever the Weather*, look for:

- words that appeal to the senses
- words that make you think of powerful images or pictures
- words that are fun to say or that sound unique
- repetition of sounds, words, or lines

SET A PURPOSE   **Ask questions** before, during, and after you read to help you get information or understand the text. Look for evidence in the text and pictures to **answer** your questions.

POWER WORDS

splatter

rumble

slather

glide

covers

creep

slithering

shimmering

Build Background: Weather and Our Feelings

Whatever the Weather

A Collection of Poems

Weather

by Eve Merriam

Dot a dot dot   dot a dot dot
Spotting the windowpane.
Spack a spack speck   flick a flack fleck
Freckling the windowpane.

A spatter a scatter   a wet cat a clatter
A splatter a rumble outside.
Umbrella umbrella umbrella umbrella
Bumbershoot barrel of rain.

Slosh a galosh   slosh a galosh
Slither and slather and glide
A puddle a jump a puddle a jump
A puddle a jump puddle splosh
A juddle a pump aluddle a dump a
Puddmuddle jump in and slide!

Covers

by Nikki Giovanni

Glass covers windows
to keep the cold away

Clouds cover the sky
to make a rainy day

Nighttime covers
all the things that creep

Blankets cover me
when I'm asleep

Cloud Dragons

by Pat Mora

What do you see
in the clouds so high?
What do you see in the sky?

Oh, I see dragons
that curl their tails
as they go slithering by.

What do you see
in the clouds so high?
What do you see? Tell me, do.

Oh, I see *caballitos*
that race the wind
high in the shimmering blue.

Turn and Talk

Use details from *Whatever the Weather* to answer these questions with a partner.

1. **Ask and Answer Questions** What questions did you ask yourself about the poems before, during, and after reading?

2. Find places in "Weather" where the poet uses repetition. How do the sounds of the words help you picture what kind of weather she is writing about?

3. Compare the settings in "Covers" and "Cloud Dragons." How does each poem make you feel?

Listening Tip

Listen carefully. Think about the meaning of what your partner says.

Write a Weather Poem

PROMPT Which of the weather poems did you like best? Choose a line, a phrase, or just a word from that poem. Use it to write your own poem about weather.

PLAN First, write the words you chose from the poem on one side of the chart. Then think of other words that describe that kind of weather. Write them on the other side of the chart.

The Poem's Words	My Words

WRITE Now put your words and the poem's words together to write a new poem about weather. Remember to:

- Think about how the words In your poem sound together.

- Use words that will help readers picture that kind of weather.

_____

_____

_____

_____

_____

_____

_____

_____

_____

_____

_____

Prepare to Read

GENRE STUDY **Poetry** uses images, sounds, and rhythm to express feelings.

MAKE A PREDICTION Preview "Weather Wonders." Think about the characteristics of poetry. What do you think you will read about in these poems?

_____

_____

_____

_____

_____

_____

SET A PURPOSE Read to see how the poems use images, sounds, and rhythm and to see if your prediction is right. If not, use what you know about poetry to make a new prediction.

Weather Wonders

READ (Circle) words that repeat. Why does the poet use repetition?

Wind

Let the wind blow. *Whoosh!*

It's all right.

I'll go out and fly my kite.

Let the wind blow. *Whee!*

I will see

Leaves blow off the maple tree.

Let the wind blow. *Wooo!*

Fancy that!

Wind just carried off my hat!

> **Close Reading Tip**
> Underline words that rhyme.

READ What is the poem mostly about? <u>Underline</u> clues that tell you.

Close Reading Tip

Put a **?** by the parts you have questions about.

Spring Sunshine

Bright sun makes me squint.

It warms my skin, melts the snow,

and opens flowers.

CHECK MY UNDERSTANDING

What words does the poet use to describe the sun?

_____

_____

_____

_____

188

WRITE ABOUT IT   Which poem do you like best? Use details
from the text to explain why.

_____

_____

_____

_____

_____

_____

_____

_____

_____

_____

Prepare to View

GENRE STUDY **Videos** are short movies that give you information or something for you to watch for enjoyment. As you watch *Rain Cloud in a Jar,* notice:

- how pictures, sounds, and words work together
- information about the topic
- the purpose of the video

SET A PURPOSE Ask yourself what happens and why to find **cause and effect** connections in the video. A cause is something that makes something else happen. An effect is what happens because of the cause.

Build Background: Clouds

Rain Cloud in a Jar

by Sci-Tech Discovery

As You View Are you ready to make it rain? Watch the experiment. Observe what happens and why. Use the words and pictures to figure out how the steps in the experiment cause something to happen. How does this help you understand rain clouds?

Use details from *Rain Cloud in a Jar* to answer these questions with a partner.

1. **Cause and Effect** What causes the shaving cream cloud to get heavier? What is the effect?

2. Why is it important to add color to the water before you drip it on the shaving cream?

3. What does observing this experiment help you understand about weather?

Talking Tip

Add your own idea to what your partner says. Be sure to use polite language.

I like your idea. My idea is _____.

Let's Wrap Up!

? **Essential Question**

How does weather affect us?

Pick one of these activities to show what you have learned about the topic.

1. My Favorite Weather

What is your favorite kind of weather? Write your opinion. Use details from the texts and from your own experiences to explain what you like about it. Draw a picture to go with your writing.

2. Reporting the Weather

Be a TV weather reporter! Choose one kind of weather to report about. Use details from the texts to describe what you see, hear, and feel. Use your voice and body to show what it is like reporting in that kind of weather!

Word Challenge

Can you use the word precipitation in your weather report?

My Notes

Glossary

A

admire [ăd-mīr′]   When you admire someone, you like and respect that person. I **admire** my friend for how he helps others.

advantages [ăd-văn′tĭj-ĕz]   Advantages are things that help put you ahead. Being a big brother has many **advantages**.

advice [ăd-vīs′]   When you give advice, you tell people what you would do. My dad gives me good **advice**.

assured [ə-shŏŏrd′]   If you assured someone, you promised something would happen. The teacher **assured** us that the bus was on the way.

average [ăv′ər-ĭj, ăv′rĭj]   Something that is average is normal or usual. My cat is smarter than the **average** pet.

C

capital [kăp′ĭ-tl]   A capital is the city where the government meets to make laws. The government building is in the **capital** city.

charge [chärj]   When you are in charge, people follow your directions. Who is in **charge** of the group?

climate [klī′mĭt]   Climate is the normal weather of a place. Some fruits grow best in a warm **climate**.

clings [klĭngz]   When something clings to something else, it sticks to it. Jane's hair **clings** to the balloon.

contraption [kən-trăp′shən]   A contraption is an object that looks strange and hard to use. Jim built an amazing flying **contraption**.

council [koun′səl]   A council is a group of people elected to lead. The members of the **council** will work together to make a decision.

covers [kŭv'ərz] Something that covers something else goes over it. Snow **covers** the yard during winter.

creep [krēp] When things creep, they move quietly and slowly. I saw the cat **creep** closer to the bird.

D

damage [dăm'ĭj] When you damage something, you cause harm to it. The storm could **damage** the old tree.

E

earned [ûrnd] If you earned something, you got what you worked for. We **earned** money by selling lemonade.

equal [ē'kwəl] Something that is equal is the same amount as something else. She divided the pie into **equal** pieces.

exactly [ĭg-zăkt'lē] When things are exactly alike, they are the same in every way. My brother and I look **exactly** alike.

excess [ĭk-sĕs', ĕk'sĕs'] An excess of something is more than is needed. Please remove any **excess** glue from the paper.

F

flash [flăsh] A flash is a sudden burst of light. The **flash** of lightning was very bright.

front [frŭnt] A cold front is where cold air meets warm air. A cold **front** will bring snow showers.

funnel [fŭn'əl] A funnel has a wide circle at the top and a short, thin tube at the bottom. She poured the mixture into the **funnel**.

G

glide [glīd] Things that glide move smoothly and easily. My new skates help me **glide** over the ice.

gusts [gŭsts] Gusts are short, strong rushes of wind. **Gusts** of wind kept blowing my umbrella inside out.

H

honored [ŏn'ərd]   When people are honored, they are praised for what they have done. Laila was **honored** for her volunteer work.

I

impressed [ĭm-prĕst']   If you are impressed, you like something a lot. She **impressed** us with her singing.

inspire [ĭn-spīr']   When people inspire you, they give you new ideas. I want to **inspire** others to be good leaders.

intent [ĭn-tĕnt']   Someone who is intent is set on doing something. The cat was **intent** on staring at the birds.

L

laws [lôz]   Laws are rules that people must follow. Our country has many important **laws**.

layer [lā'ər]   If you have on more than one layer of clothing, you are wearing several things on top of one another to keep warm. I always put on more than one **layer** of clothes on snowy days.

M

members [mĕm'bərz]   Members are people who belong to a group. The other **members** of government welcomed the new senator.

O

occur [ə-kûr']   When things happen or take place, they occur. The graduation party will **occur** as soon as the ceremony is over.

P

peered [pîrd]   If you peered, you looked closely. Sofi and Diana **peered** into the microscope at the drop of pond water.

pellets [pĕl'ĭts]   Pellets are tiny balls of something. Savannah brushed her pet rabbit and gave it some food **pellets**.

pioneer [pī'ə-nîr']   When you pioneer something, you are the first person to do it. Astronauts help us **pioneer** new ways of exploring outer space.

politics [pŏl'ĭ-tĭks]   Politics is the work done by people in government. Helping people in his community was his favorite part of working in **politics**.

precipitation [prĭ-sĭp'ĭ-tā'shən]   Precipitation is water that falls from the sky, such as rain, sleet, hail, or snow. The weather report shows a strong chance of **precipitation**.

precise [prĭ-sīs']   Something that is precise is exact and correct. She gave us precise directions to the park.

predict [prĭ-dĭkt']   If you predict something, you say it will happen before it does. I **predict** that it will be sunny tomorrow.

R

rare [râr]   Something that is rare does not happen often. It is **rare** for my brother to clean up his room.

relay [rē'lā]   A relay is a team race where each member runs one part of it. It takes teamwork to win a **relay** race.

replica [rĕp'lĭ-kə]   A replica is an exact copy of something. Each cookie was a **replica** of the other.

respond [rĭ-spŏnd']   When you respond, you answer in some way. I do not know how to **respond** to your question.

rumble [rŭm'bəl]   A rumble is a long, booming noise. We heard a **rumble** of thunder.

S

shimmering [shĭm'ər-ĭng]   Something that is shimmering is shining. The silver confetti was **shimmering** in Jem's hands at the party.

slather [slăth'ər]   If you slather something, you put a lot of it over something else. Let me **slather** this sunscreen on your face before we go to the beach.

slithering [slĭth'ər-ĭng]   If something is slithering by, it is sliding past. We saw a snake **slithering** through the grass.

solve [sŏlv, sôlv]   When you solve a problem, you find an answer to it. I want to **solve** this math problem.

splatter [splăt'ər]   When things splatter, drops fall out of them. If you aren't careful, paint will **splatter** on the floor.

state [stāt]   A state is an area of land that is part of a country and has its own government. We will visit the **state** of Florida.

success [sək-sĕs']   Success is when you finish something you worked hard to do. Our talent show was a big **success**.

supplies [sə-plīz']   Supplies are the things people need to be ready for something. I have all the **supplies** I need for the storm.

T

temperature [tĕm'pər-ə-choor', tĕm'pər-ə-chər, tĕm'prə-choor', tĕm'prə-chər]   Temperature is how hot or cold a place is. How cold is the **temperature** today?

tough [tŭf]   If something is tough to do, it is difficult or challenging. It was a very **tough** choice so we decided to get both kittens.

troop [troop]   A troop is a group of people who belong to a club. My friends and I are in the same girls' **troop** at school.

Index of Titles and Authors

Acknowledgments

"Cloud Dragons" from *Confetti: Poems for Children* by Pat Mora. Text copyright © 1996 by Pat Mora. Reprinted by permission of Lee & Low Books Inc.

Cloudette by Tom Lichtenheld. Copyright © 2011 by Tom Lichtenheld. Reprinted by arrangement with Henry Holt Books for Young Readers.

"Covers" From *The Sun Is So Quiet* by Nikki Giovanni. Text copyright © 1996 by Nikki Giovanni. Reprinted by permission of Henry Holt Books for Young Readers.

Going Places by Peter and Paul Reynolds. Text copyright © 2014 by Peter H. Reynolds and Paul A. Reynolds. Illustrations copyright © 2014 by Peter H. Reynolds. Reprinted by permission of Atheneum Books For Young Readers, an Imprint of Simon & Schuster Children's Publishing Division, and Pippin Properties, Inc.

"Weather" from *Catch a Little Rhyme* by Eve Merriam. Text copyright © 1966, renewed © 1994 by Eve Merriam. Reprinted by permission of Marian Reiner.

Excerpt from *Who Are Government's Leaders?* by Jennifer Boothroyd. Text copyright © 2016 by Lerner Publishing Group, Inc. Reprinted by permission of Lerner Publications Company, a division of Lerner Publishing Group, Inc.

Wild Weather by Thomas Kingsley Troupe, illustrated by Jamey Christoph.

Copyright © 2014 by Picture Window Books, a Capstone imprint. Reprinted by permission of Capstone Press Publishers.

Wilma Rudolph: Against All Odds by Stephanie E. Macceca. Text copyright © 2011 by Teacher Created Materials, Inc. Reprinted by permission of Teacher Created Materials, Inc.

Credits